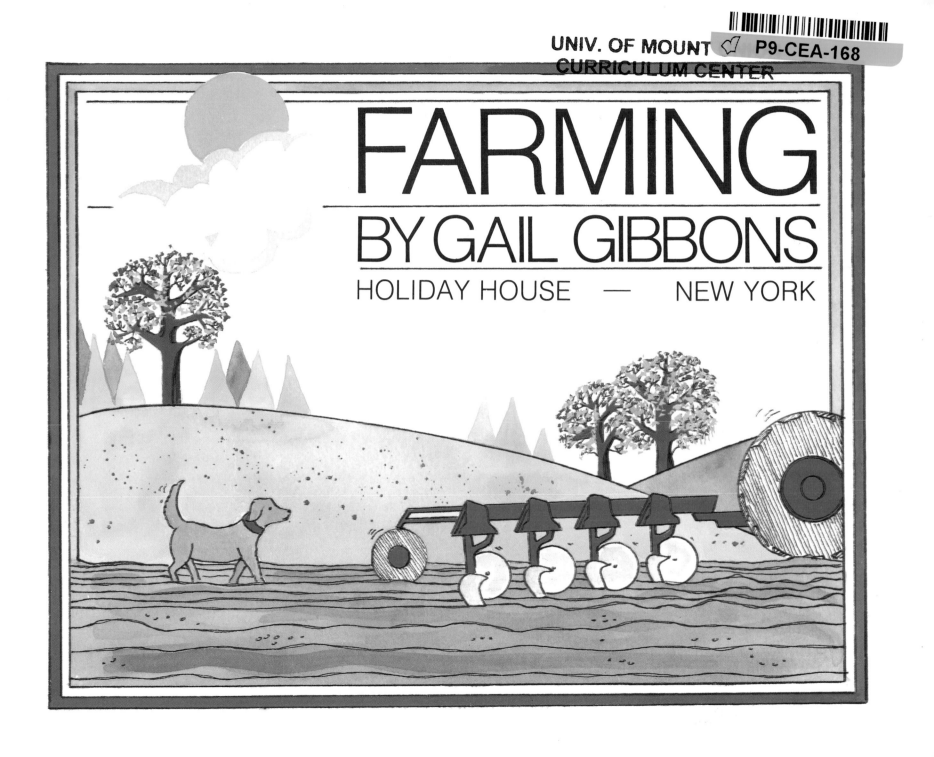

FARMING

BY GAIL GIBBONS

HOLIDAY HOUSE — NEW YORK

Special thanks to Maxine and Gregory Slack
of Corinth, VT; Rudy Martin of M&M Motors,
Montpelier, VT; J. S. Woodhouse Co., West
Springfield, MA; and Townline Equipment Sales,
Plainfield, NH

Library of Congress Cataloging-in-Publication Data

Gibbons, Gail.
Farming.

Summary: An introduction, in simple text and
illustrations, to farming and the work done on a
farm throughout the seasons.
1. Agriculture – Juvenile literature.   2. Farm life –
Juvenile literature.   3. Farms – Juvenile literature.
[1. Farms.   2. Farm life]   I. Title.
S519.G53   1988   630   87-21254
ISBN 0-8234-0682-2
ISBN 0-8234-0797-7 (pbk.)

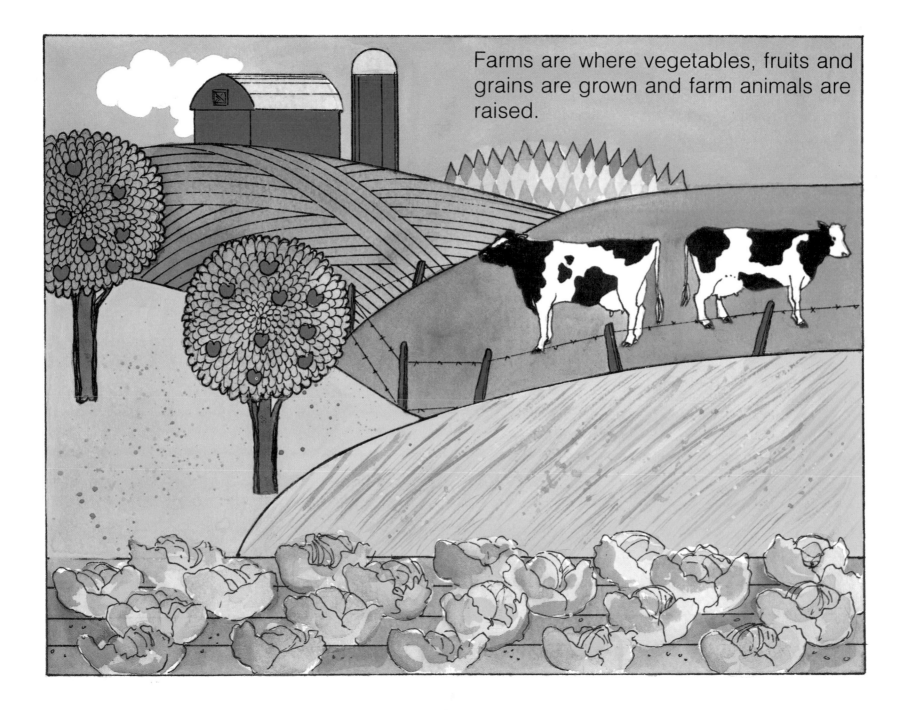

Farms are where vegetables, fruits and grains are grown and farm animals are raised.

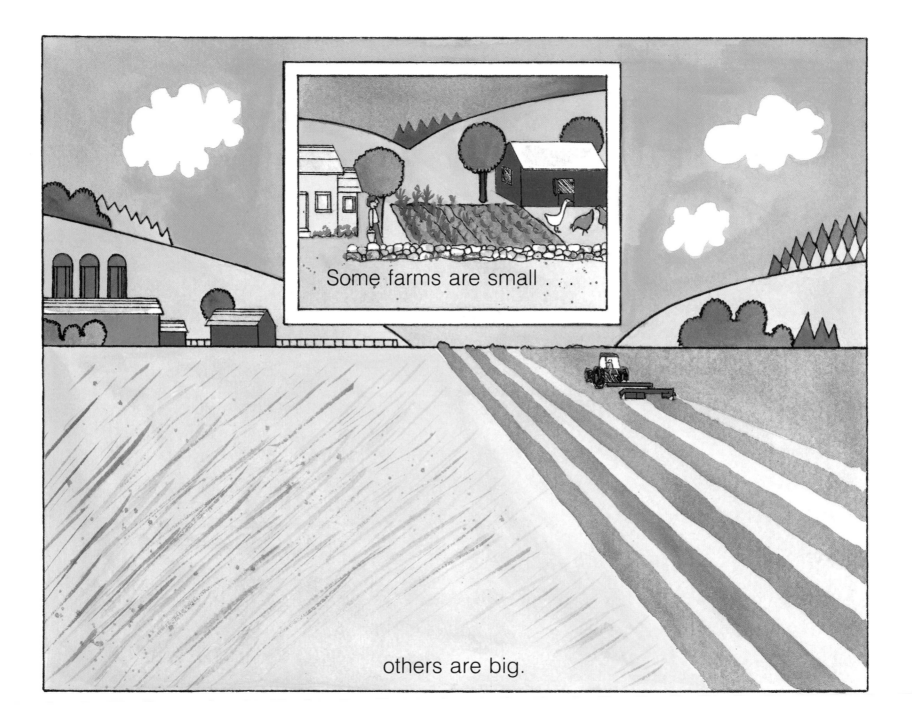

Some farms are small . . . .

others are big.

Most farms are owned by families.
They are busy places throughout the year.

Spring on the farm.

The days become longer.

Geese fly north.

Green leaves begin to appear on branches.

Baby chicks are brought to the chicken house.

silo

barn

chicken house

machine shed

farmhouse

There are baby lambs to check on in the barn.

The temperature climbs on the porch thermometer.

farm stand

Ice breaks up on the farm pond.

Spring flowers poke through the ground.

Outside chores . . .

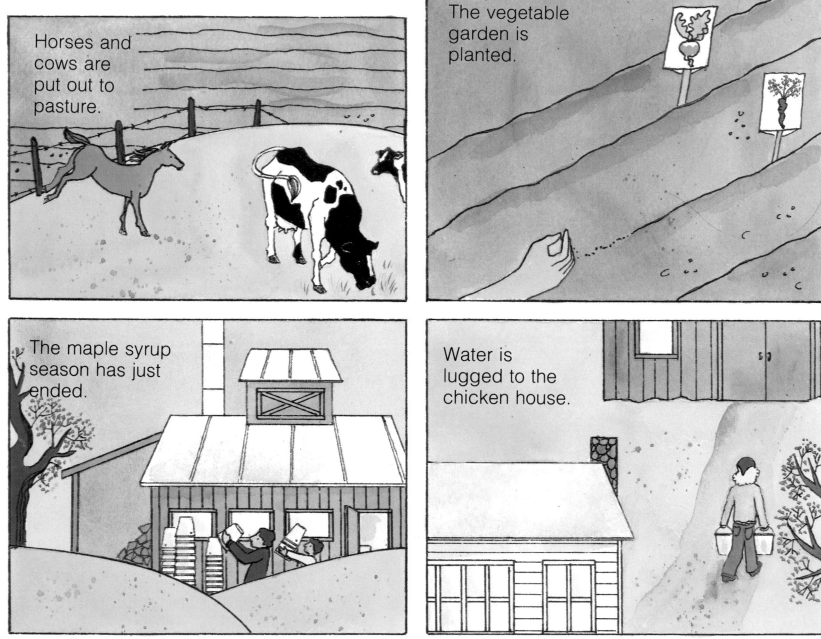

Horses and cows are put out to pasture.

The vegetable garden is planted.

The maple syrup season has just ended.

Water is lugged to the chicken house.

and inside chores.

The stalls are always being cleaned.

The new baby chicks need constant care.

There are new farm babies.

The cows are milked in the morning and in the evening.

Summer on the farm.

It is hot.

beehives

Bees collect nectar from flowers to make honey.

The garden is hoed.

Vegetables grow in the garden.

Time to go swimming!

Flowers bloom.

The hay grows tall.

The corn grows tall.

The baby animals are bigger now.

Cows munch grass.

Outside chores . . .

Some vegetables
are gathered.

Honey is
collected.

and inside chores.

Vegetables are canned or frozen.

canning jars

Eggs are collected each day of the year.

The vet gives a calf a checkup.

The cows are milked twice a day every day of the year.

The hay is put in the hayloft.

Fall on the farm.

Geese fly south.

The days become shorter.

The leaves turn gold and orange.

The pumpkins are big and round.

FRESH CORN

The apples
are red.

The corn
is very
tall.

The farm
babies are
big now.

It is cool
outside. Soon
there will be
a frost.

Outside chores . . .

After morning chores, it's time to go to school.

Eggs are packed for delivery.

At the end of the growing season, all fruits and vegetables are harvested.

The cornfields are harvested.

harvester

The silo is filled with chopped corn. The corn and hay will feed the animals through the winter.

The hayloft is packed solid.

and inside chores.

Bushels of apples have been put in the farmstand.

Canned foods line the shelves.

Some animals are going to market to be sold.

The cows' milk is sold to a dairy throughout the year.

Winter on the farm.

The days
are short.

Footprints
lead to
the barn.

Ice is on
the pond.

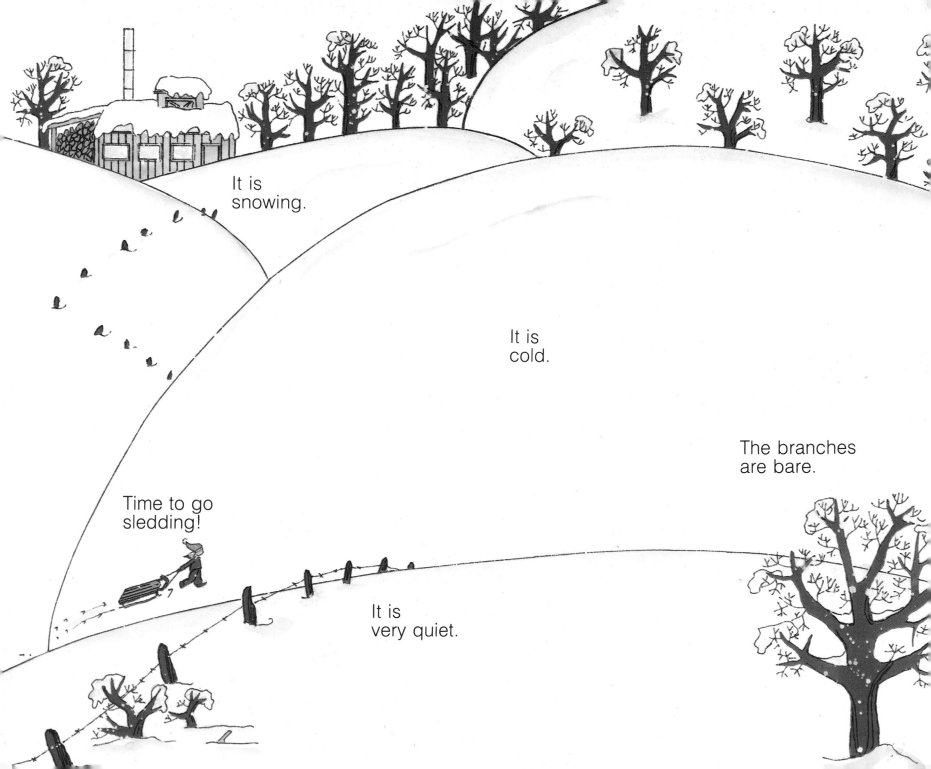

It is
snowing.

It is
cold.

The branches
are bare.

Time to go
sledding!

It is
very quiet.

Outside chores . . .

The road
is plowed.

Water is
carried to
the chicken
house.

and inside chores.

Farm machinery is repaired and cleaned.

The cows are milked.

There is plenty of hay and grain to eat.

All the animals are inside for the cold winter.

Last summer's vegetables simmer in a pot.

Bookkeeping and plans for next year's crops are worked on.

KINDS OF FARMING

Most farms are specialized. They produce one or two main crops or kinds of farm animals.

DAIRY FARMS

Dairy farms raise dairy cows for their milk. The milk is sold to dairies where it is processed and packaged.

EGG AND POULTRY FARMS

Egg farms raise chickens to lay eggs. Poultry farms raise chickens for their meat.

GRAIN FARMS

Grain farms grow grain for making bread and cereals and other foods.
Some grains are grown for animals, too.

FRUIT FARMS

Fruit farms grow apples, peaches, oranges and other fruits for people to eat.

VEGETABLE FARMS

Vegetable farms grow beans, lettuce, carrots and other vegetables. They are sent to market and stores to be sold.

CATTLE FARMS AND RANCHES

Beef cattle, pigs and other animals are raised for their meat.